The Frugal Millionaire

"Secrets to Building Wealth on a Budget"

Disclaimer

Before reading this book, it's important you know that all content included in this book is 100% generated by an Artificial Intelligence and has been reviewed by the Author.

The author and publisher shall not be liable for any errors or omissions in the book or for any actions taken based on the information contained in this book. The reader is encouraged to seek professional financial advice before making any financial decisions.

By reading this book, you acknowledge and agree that the author and publisher shall not be held liable for any actions taken or not taken based on the information contained in this book. This disclaimer applies to all information contained in this book and any related materials.

Dedication

To all the frugal millionaires out there, past, present, and future:

This book is dedicated to you and the pursuit of financial success and independence. Building wealth on a budget takes time, effort, and persistence, but with the right strategies and mindset, anything is possible. Thank you for your dedication and determination to achieve your financial goals and live a fulfilling, financially responsible life. May this book serve as a guide and inspiration on your journey towards financial success.

Legal Notice

The Frugal Millionaire: Secrets to Building Wealth on a Budget is a work of non-fiction. While some of the examples and case studies included in this book are based on real events, they have been modified and adapted to fit the purposes of this book. Any resemblance to actual persons, living or dead, or events is purely coincidental.

The information contained in this book is for general information purposes only. It is not intended to be a substitute for professional financial advice and should not be relied upon as such. The author and publisher make no representation or warranties of any kind, express or implied, about the completeness, accuracy, reliability, suitability, or availability with respect to the book or the information, products, services, or related graphics contained in the book for any purpose. Any reliance you place on such information is therefore strictly at your own risk.

The author and publisher shall not be liable for any errors or omissions in the book or for any actions taken based on the information contained in this book. The reader is encouraged to seek professional financial advice before making any financial decisions.

This book is not intended to promote any specific financial products or services and the author and publisher do not receive any financial compensation for the inclusion of any products or services in this book. The author and publisher have no affiliation with any financial products or services mentioned in this book.

The views and opinions expressed in this book are those of the author and do not necessarily reflect the views of the publisher. The publisher and author do not endorse any products or services mentioned in this book.

By reading this book, you agree to the terms and conditions outlined in this legal notice. If you do not agree to these terms and conditions, please do not continue reading this book.

Table of Contents

Disclaimer

Dedication

Legal Notice

Introduction

- Definition of frugal millionaire
- Importance of budgeting in building wealth
- Common misconceptions about frugality and wealth

The Fundamentals of Frugal Living

- Setting Financial Goals and Creating a Budget
- Cutting Expenses and Finding Ways to Save Money
- Prioritizing Your Spending and Avoiding Financial Pitfalls

Investing for the Long-Term

- Understanding the Different Types of Investments
- Developing a Diversified Investment Portfolio
- The Importance of Compound Interest and Long-Term Planning

Building Multiple Streams of Income

- The Benefits of Having Multiple Sources of Income

- Finding Ways to Earn Passive Income
- Tips for Starting a Side Hustle or Small Business

Staying Motivated and Focused on Your Financial Goals

- Overcoming Financial Setbacks and Challenges
- Tips for Staying Motivated and Committed to Your Financial Plan
- The Importance of Accountability and Support

Conclusion

- Recap of key points and takeaways
- Encouragement to take action and start building wealth on a budget
- Final thoughts on the benefits of living a frugal and financially responsible lifestyle

Introduction

Are you tired of living pay-check to pay-check, struggling to make ends meet and save for the future? Do you dream of financial freedom and the ability to retire comfortably, but feel like it's an unattainable goal? If so, you're not alone. Many people struggle with managing their money and building wealth, especially in today's fast-paced, consumer-driven society.

But what if I told you that it's possible to build wealth and achieve financial independence, even on a tight budget? That's right – it is possible to be a millionaire without breaking the bank or living extravagantly. In this book, "The Frugal Millionaire: Secrets to Building Wealth on a Budget," we'll explore the principles and practices of frugal living and how they can help you build a solid financial foundation and reach your financial goals.

You may be wondering what a "frugal millionaire" even is. Simply put, it's someone who has mastered the art of living below their means and saving and investing wisely, allowing them to accumulate wealth over time. Frugal millionaires understand that building wealth is not about how much money you make, but rather how you manage and grow the money you have.

In the following chapters, we'll delve into the fundamentals of frugal living and how to cut expenses and find ways to save money. We'll also explore the importance of investing for the long-term and developing multiple streams of income. Along the way, we'll offer tips and strategies for staying motivated and focused on your financial goals, and overcoming any setbacks or challenges you may encounter.

By the end of this book, you'll have the tools and knowledge you need to start building wealth on a budget and take control of your financial future. So, let's get started!

• Definition of frugal millionaire

A frugal millionaire is someone who has mastered the art of living below their means and saving and investing wisely, allowing them to accumulate wealth over time. Frugal millionaires understand that building wealth is not about how much money you make, but rather how you manage and grow the money you have. They are able to live a fulfilling and comfortable lifestyle while also being mindful of their spending and saving habits. They are able to achieve financial independence and reach their financial goals through a combination of frugal living, smart investing, and building multiple streams of income. Frugal millionaires are not defined by their income or their possessions, but rather by their ability to live within their means and make their money work for them.

• Importance of budgeting in building wealth

Budgeting is a crucial tool for building wealth and achieving financial independence because it allows you to take control of your finances and make informed decisions about where your money is going. By creating a budget, you can clearly see how much money you have coming in and going out, and make adjustments as needed to ensure that you are saving and investing enough to reach your financial goals.

One of the key benefits of budgeting is that it helps you to prioritize your spending and identify areas where you may be able to cut back or save money. By allocating your money towards your most important financial goals and needs, you can make sure that you are using your resources effectively and efficiently. This can help you to avoid financial pitfalls and make the most of your money.

In addition to helping to you save and invest for the future, budgeting can also reduce stress and increase financial security. When you have a clear understanding of your financial situation and a plan in place, it can give you peace of mind and help you feel more in control of your financial life. This can be especially important in times of economic uncertainty or financial hardship.

Another reason why budgeting is so important for building wealth is that it allows you to set financial goals and track your progress towards achieving them. By setting clear, specific goals and creating a budget that aligns with those goals, you can stay motivated and on track. This can help you to stay focused and avoid getting sidetracked or losing sight of your financial priorities.

Finally, budgeting can help you to build an emergency fund and prepare for unexpected expenses. By setting aside a portion of your budget for emergencies, you can be better equipped to handle unexpected expenses and avoid having to borrow money or go into debt. This can give you peace of mind and help you to feel more financially secure.

- ## Common misconceptions about frugality and wealth

There are a few common misconceptions about frugality and wealth that we'd like to address:

1. Frugality means living a miserable, ascetic lifestyle. Many people believe that being frugal means depriving oneself of pleasure and living a miserly, unfulfilling life. However, this is not necessarily the case. Frugal living can actually be quite enjoyable and fulfilling, as it allows you to focus on the things that truly matter to you and spend your money on the things that bring you the most value and happiness.

2. You have to be rich to be frugal. Some people assume that only wealthy individuals can afford to be frugal, as they have the financial resources to

save money and invest wisely. However, this is not necessarily true. Frugal living is about managing your money effectively and maximizing your resources, regardless of your income level. By being mindful of your spending and finding ways to save money, you can build wealth and achieve financial independence, no matter what your income is.

3. Frugality means being cheap and stingy. Some people associate frugality with being cheap or stingy, but this is not the case. Frugal living is about making smart financial decisions and maximizing the value of your money, not about being miserly or unwilling to spend money on things that matter to you. By being mindful of your spending and prioritizing your financial goals, you can live a fulfilling and comfortable

life while also building wealth and achieving financial independence.

The Fundamentals of Frugal Living

In order to build wealth and achieve financial independence, it's important to master the art of frugal living. Frugal living is about maximizing the value of your money and making smart financial decisions that allow you to save and invest for the future. In this chapter, we'll delve into the fundamentals of frugal living and how you can apply these principles to your own financial life.

- ## Setting Financial Goals and Creating a Budget

The first step to successful frugal living is setting financial goals and creating a budget. By setting clear, specific financial goals, you can have a roadmap to guide your financial decisions and stay motivated and on track. Some common financial goals might include saving for a down payment on a home, paying off debt, building an emergency fund, or saving for retirement.

It's important to be realistic and specific when setting financial goals. Instead of setting a vague goal like "saving more money," try setting a specific, measurable goal like "saving $20,000 for a down payment on a home within the next five years." This will give you a clear target to work towards and help you to stay motivated and on track.

Once you have your financial goals in place, the next step is to create a budget that aligns with those goals. A budget is a plan for how you will allocate your income and expenses in order to reach your financial goals. There are many different ways to create a budget, and the right approach will depend on your personal financial situation and needs. Some common budgeting methods include the 50/30/20 rule (allocating 50% of your budget to needs, 30% to wants, and 20% to savings and debt repayment), the envelope method (allocating a set amount of money to different spending categories in envelopes), or the zero-sum budget (allocating every dollar of income to a specific category).

To create a budget, start by taking a close look at your income and expenses. Write down all of your sources of income, including your salary, any side hustle income, and any other sources of income. Then, make a list of all of your expenses, including fixed expenses like rent or mortgage payments, and variable expenses like groceries and entertainment. Be as thorough as possible when listing your expenses, as it's important to have a complete picture of your financial situation.

Once you have a list of your income and expenses, it's time to start allocating your money towards your financial goals. This will involve creating a plan for how you will spend and save your money each month. Depending on your financial goals and needs, you may need to cut back on certain expenses in order to allocate more money.

- Cutting Expenses and Finding Ways to Save Money

Once you have your budget in place, the next step is to start looking for ways to cut expenses and save money. There are many different ways to do this, and it will depend on your personal financial situation and spending habits. Some common strategies for saving money include:

Cutting unnecessary expenses: Take a close look at your budget and identify any expenses that are non-essential or that you can live without. By cutting these expenses, you can free up money to put towards your financial goals.

Negotiating lower rates: If you have credit card debt, student loans, or other debts with high interest rates, consider negotiating with your creditors to get a lower rate. This can save you a significant amount of money over time.

Shopping around for better deals: Before making a purchase, take the time to shop around and compare prices to ensure that you are getting the best deal possible. This can also apply to things like insurance premiums, cell phone plans, and other recurring expenses.

Building a price comparison tool: Consider creating a price comparison tool to help you track the best prices for items that you regularly purchase. This can help you to save money over time by ensuring that you are always getting the best deal.

Reducing energy costs: Look for ways to reduce your energy costs, such as by using energy-efficient appliances, turning off lights and electronics when not in use, and sealing windows and doors to prevent drafts.

Cooking at home: Instead of eating out or ordering takeout, try cooking at home more often; This can be a great way to save money.

- ## Prioritizing Your Spending and Avoiding Financial Pitfalls

In addition to cutting expenses and finding ways to save money, it's also important to prioritize your spending and make sure that you are allocating your money towards your most important financial goals. This means being mindful of your spending habits and avoiding financial pitfalls that can derail your progress towards financial independence.

Some common financial pitfalls to avoid include:

Impulse spending: It's easy to get caught up in the excitement of a sale or a new product and make a purchase on impulse. To avoid this, try to take a step back and consider whether you really need the item and whether it aligns with your financial goals.

Keeping up with the Joneses: It's natural to want to keep up with the latest trends and have the same material possessions as our peers, but this can be a recipe for financial disaster. Instead of trying to compete with others, focus on your own financial goals and priorities and make sure that your spending aligns with those goals.

Paying high fees: Many financial products and services come with hidden fees that can eat into your wealth. To avoid paying high fees, be sure to do your research and shop around for the best deals on things like credit cards, bank accounts, and investment products.

Going into debt: Credit can be a useful tool, but it's important to use it wisely. Avoid going into debt unless it is absolutely necessary and make sure to pay off your debts as soon as possible to avoid accruing high interest charges.

By being mindful of your spending and avoiding financial pitfalls, you can make the most of your money and stay on track towards achieving your financial goals.

Investing for the Long-Term

One of the key principles of frugal living and building wealth is investing for the long-term. By investing in a diversified portfolio of assets, you can grow your wealth over time and achieve financial independence. In this chapter, we'll explore the basics of investing and how you can get started building a long-term investment plan.

The Benefits of Investing for the Long-Term

Investing for the long-term has a number of benefits, including:

1. Compound interest: One of the biggest advantages of investing for the long-term is the power of compound interest. When you invest money, it earns interest, which is then reinvested and earns even more interest. This creates a snowball effect that can significantly increase your wealth over time.

2. Diversification: By investing in a diverse portfolio of assets, you can reduce your risk and increase your chances of success. Diversification can help to protect your portfolio from market downturns and increase your

chances of achieving your financial goals.

3. Professional management: Many investment products, such as mutual funds and exchange-traded funds (ETFs), are professionally managed by experts who can help you to make informed investment decisions. This can be especially helpful for those who are new to investing or who don't have the time or expertise to manage their own investments.

Getting Started with Investing

If you're new to investing, it can be intimidating to get started. Here are some steps you can take to get started building a long-term investment plan:

1. Set financial goals: Before you start investing, it's important to have a clear idea of your financial goals. What do you want to achieve with your investments? Do you want to save for retirement, build an emergency fund, or buy a home? By setting specific, measurable financial goals, you'll have a roadmap to guide your investment decisions.

2. Assess your risk tolerance: Different investments carry different levels of risk. Before you start investing, it's important to assess your risk tolerance and determine how much risk you are comfortable taking on. This will help you to choose investments that align with your financial goals and risk tolerance.

3. Build a diversified portfolio: Once you have an idea of your financial goals and risk tolerance, it's time to start building a diversified portfolio of assets. This might include stocks, bonds, mutual funds, ETFs, and other investment products. It's important to diversify your portfolio in order to reduce your risk and increase your chances of success.

4. Review and rebalance your portfolio: It's important to periodically review and rebalance your portfolio to ensure that it aligns with your financial goals and risk tolerance. This might involve selling off underperforming assets and buying new ones to maintain a balance.

- ## Understanding the Different Types of Investments

When it comes to investing for the long-term, there are many different types of investments to choose from. Some common types of investments include:

1. Stocks: Stocks, also known as equities, are shares of ownership in a company. When you buy a stock, you are buying a small piece of the company and becoming a shareholder. Stocks can be risky, as their value can fluctuate significantly depending on the performance of the company and the overall stock market. However, they can also offer the potential for high returns over the long-term.

2. Bonds: Bonds are debt securities that are issued by companies, municipalities, and other organizations. When you buy a bond, you are essentially lending money to the issuer in exchange for interest payments. Bonds are generally considered to be less risky than stocks, but they also tend to offer lower returns.

3. Mutual funds: Mutual funds are investment vehicles that pool together money from many different investors and use it to buy a diversified portfolio of stocks, bonds, and other assets. Mutual funds are managed by professional fund managers and offer the benefits of diversification and professional management.

4. Exchange-traded funds (ETFs): ETFs are similar to mutual funds in that they offer a diversified portfolio of assets, but they are traded like stocks on an exchange. ETFs are generally considered to be more tax-efficient than mutual funds and can offer lower fees.

5. Real estate: Investing in real estate can be a great way to diversify your portfolio and potentially earn passive income. There are many different ways to invest in real estate, including buying rental properties, flipping houses, or investing in real estate investment trusts (REITs).

It's Important to do your research and understand the risks and potential rewards of different investments before making any decisions. By diversifying your portfolio and investing for the long-term, you can increase your chances of achieving your financial goals and building wealth.

- ## Developing a Diversified Investment Portfolio

One of the keys to successful long-term investing is building a diversified portfolio. A diversified portfolio is one that is spread out across different types of assets and industries in order to reduce risk and increase the chances of success. By diversifying your portfolio, you can protect yourself against market downturns and increase your chances of achieving your financial goals.

There are many different ways to build a diversified portfolio, and the right approach will depend on your financial goals, risk tolerance, and investment horizon. Some common strategies for building a diversified portfolio include:

Asset allocation: Asset allocation is the process of dividing your investment portfolio among different asset classes, such as stocks, bonds, and cash. By allocating your assets among different asset classes, you can reduce your risk and increase your chances of success.

Diversification within asset classes: In addition to diversifying across different asset classes, it's also important to diversify within each asset class. For example, if you are investing in stocks, you might consider diversifying among different sectors, such as technology, healthcare, and energy.

Geographic diversification: Another way to diversify your portfolio is by investing in assets from different geographic regions. This can help to protect your portfolio from economic and political events in any one region.

Dollar-cost averaging: Dollar-cost averaging is a strategy that involves investing a fixed amount of money at regular intervals, rather than investing a lump sum all at once. This can help to smooth out the effects of market fluctuations and reduce the risk of investing at the wrong time.

By developing a diversified investment portfolio, you can increase your chances of success and protect your wealth over the long-term. It's important to regularly review and rebalance your portfolio to ensure that it remains aligned with your financial goals and risk tolerance.

- ## The Importance of Compound Interest and Long-Term Planning

One of the key benefits of investing for the long-term is the power of compound interest. Compound interest is the interest that is earned on the principal of an investment, as well as on any accumulated interest. This creates a snowball effect that can significantly increase your wealth over time.

For example, let's say you invest $1,000 at a 6% annual interest rate. After one year, your investment will be worth $1,060 (1000 x

1.06). If you leave the money invested for another year, it will earn an additional 6% interest, bringing the total value to $1,123.60 (1060 x 1.06). As you can see, the longer you leave your money invested, the more it grows through compound interest.

The key to taking advantage of compound interest is to start investing as early as possible and to be consistent with your investments. By investing early and consistently, you can take advantage of the power of compound interest and build significant wealth over time.

In addition to the power of compound interest, long-term planning is also important for successful investing. By setting clear, specific financial goals and creating a long-term investment plan, you can stay focused and on track towards achieving your goals. This might involve setting up automatic investments, creating a budget, and regularly reviewing and adjusting your portfolio to ensure that it aligns with your goals.

By taking advantage of compound interest and engaging in long-term planning, you can increase your chances of success and build wealth over time. So, it is very important to invest early and consistently in order to take the full advantage of compound interest and long-term planning.

Building Multiple Streams of Income

Another key principle of frugal living and building wealth is building multiple streams of income. By diversifying your income sources, you can reduce your financial risk and increase your chances of achieving financial independence. In this chapter, we'll explore the benefits of building multiple streams of income and some strategies for doing so.

- ## The Benefits of Having Multiple Sources of Income

Having multiple sources of income can provide many benefits to those who are working towards financial independence and building wealth. Some of the key benefits of having multiple sources of income include:

Financial stability: By having multiple sources of income, you can reduce your financial risk and increase your chances of financial stability. If one source of income dries up, you'll have others to fall back on. This can be especially important in times of economic uncertainty or during periods of unexpected financial setbacks.

Increased earning potential: Building multiple streams of income can also increase your overall earning potential. By adding additional sources of income, you can potentially earn more money and reach your financial goals faster.

Flexibility: Having multiple streams of income can also give you more flexibility in your career and financial decisions. For example, you might be able to take on a lower-paying job that you enjoy more, knowing that you have other sources of income to support you. This can be especially helpful for those who are looking to change careers or pursue their passions.

Diversification: Diversifying your income sources can also help to protect you from economic downturns and market fluctuations. By having a mix of income sources, you can reduce your risk and increase your chances of success.

By building multiple streams of income, you can increase your financial stability and flexibility and take control of your financial future. It's important to regularly review and assess your income streams to ensure that they are aligned with your financial goals and risk tolerance.

- ## Finding Ways to Earn Passive Income

One of the key strategies for building multiple streams of income is to find ways to earn passive income. Passive income is income that is earned without requiring active participation or effort. Some common ways to earn passive income include:

Investing in rental properties: Investing in rental properties can be a great way to earn passive income. By owning rental properties, you can earn passive income from the rent paid by tenants. It's important to do your research and understand the risks and responsibilities of being a landlord before diving into real estate investing.

Selling digital products: Digital products, such as eBooks, courses, and software, can be a great way to earn passive income. By creating and selling digital products, you can reach a global market and earn passive income while you sleep.

Investing in dividend-paying stocks: Some stocks pay dividends, which are periodic payments to shareholders. By investing in dividend-paying stocks, you can earn passive income in the form of dividends.

Creating a blog or YouTube channel: By creating a blog or YouTube channel and monetizing it through advertising, sponsorships, and other methods, you can earn passive income from your content.

Investing in peer-to-peer lending platforms: Peer-to-peer lending platforms, such as Lending Club and Prosper, allow investors to lend money to borrowers in exchange for interest payments. By investing in peer-to-peer lending platforms, you can earn passive income in the form of interest payments.

It's Important to keep in mind that earning passive income is not always easy and may require upfront work and investment in order to generate returns. However, by finding ways to earn passive income, you can increase your financial stability and flexibility and take control of your financial future.

- ## Tips for Starting a Side Hustle or Small Business

Starting a side hustle or small business can be a great way to build multiple streams of income and increase your earning potential. Here are some tips to help you get started:

Find a niche: The key to success in any business is to find a niche and offer something unique or valuable to your customers. Take some time to research your market and identify a need or opportunity that you can fill.

Validate your idea: Before you invest a lot of time and money into your side hustle or small business, it's important to validate your idea. This might involve conducting market research, creating a minimum viable product (MVP), or testing your idea with a small group of customers.

Create a plan: Once you have a clear idea of your business, it's important to create a plan that outlines your goals, target market, pricing, and marketing strategies. A business plan can help you to stay focused and on track as you work to build your business.

Build a team: Building a team of advisors, mentors, and partners can be a great way to accelerate the growth of your side hustle or small business. Look for people who have complementary skills and expertise and who can help you to achieve your goals.

Stay focused and be persistent: Starting a side hustle or small business requires hard work, dedication, and persistence. It's important to stay focused on your goals and be willing to put in the time and effort required to succeed.

By following these tips, you can increase your chances of success and build a sustainable side hustle or small business.

Staying Motivated and Focused on Your Financial Goals

One of the keys to achieving financial success is staying motivated and focused on your financial goals. It can be easy to get side-tracked or lose motivation along the way, but by setting clear goals and developing a plan to achieve them, you can increase your chances of success. In this chapter, we'll explore some strategies for staying motivated and focused on your financial goals.

Set Clear, Specific Goals

The first step to staying motivated and focused on your financial goals is to set clear, specific goals. This means identifying exactly what you want to achieve and setting a timeline for achieving it. For example, instead of setting a vague goal like "save more money," you might set a specific goal like "save $20,000 for a down payment on a house within the next two years." By setting specific goals, you can create a roadmap for achieving them and stay motivated along the way.

Create a Plan and Take Action

Once you have set your financial goals, it's important to create a plan for achieving them and take action. This might involve creating a budget, setting up automatic investments, or finding ways to increase your income. By taking small, consistent steps towards your goals, you can stay focused and motivated and increase your chances of success.

Track Your Progress

Tracking your progress can be a great way to stay motivated and on track towards achieving your financial goals. This might involve creating a spreadsheet to track your spending, saving, and investing or using financial tracking tools such as Mint or Personal Capital. By regularly reviewing your progress, you can stay focused and motivated and make any necessary adjustments to your plan.

Seek Support and Encouragement

It can be helpful to seek support and encouragement from friends, family, or a financial professional as you work towards your financial goals. Surrounding yourself with supportive people can help to keep you motivated and on track and provide you with valuable insights and guidance.

By setting clear, specific financial goals, creating a plan, tracking your progress, and seeking support and encouragement, you can increase your chances of success and stay motivated and focused on your financial goals. So, it is very important to stay motivated and focused on your financial goals in order to achieve them.

• Overcoming Financial Setbacks and Challenges

No matter how carefully you plan, it's likely that you'll encounter financial setbacks and challenges at some point in your journey towards financial independence. It's important to remember that these setbacks and challenges are a normal part of the process and can be opportunities for growth and learning. Here are some strategies for overcoming financial setbacks and challenges:

Keep perspective: It's important to keep things in perspective and remember that financial setbacks and challenges are often temporary. While it can be frustrating or difficult to deal with financial setbacks, it's important to keep a long-term perspective and stay focused on your goals.

Seek support and guidance: If you're facing financial setbacks or challenges, it can be helpful to seek support and guidance from friends, family, or a financial professional. These individuals can provide you with valuable insights, encouragement, and guidance as you work to overcome your challenges.

Adjust your plan: If you're facing financial setbacks or challenges, it might be necessary to adjust your financial plan in order to get back on track. This might involve cutting expenses, finding ways to increase your income, or adjusting your goals.

Learn from your mistakes: Financial setbacks and challenges can be opportunities for learning and growth. Take some time to reflect on what led to the setback or challenge and what you can do differently in the future to avoid similar situations.

Stay motivated and focused: It's important to stay motivated and focused on your financial goals, even when you're facing setbacks or challenges. Remember why you set your financial goals in the first place and keep working towards them.

By keeping perspective, seeking support and guidance, adjusting your plan, learning from your mistakes, and staying motivated and focused, you can overcome financial setbacks and challenges and continue working towards your financial goals.

- ## Tips for Staying Motivated and Committed to Your Financial Plan

Staying motivated and committed to your financial plan can be challenging, especially if you're facing setbacks or challenges. Here are some tips to help you stay motivated and on track:

Set clear, specific goals: The first step to staying motivated and committed to your financial plan is to set clear, specific goals. This means identifying exactly what you want to achieve and setting a timeline for achieving it. By setting specific goals, you can create a roadmap for achieving them and stay motivated along the way.

Celebrate your progress: It's important to celebrate your progress and accomplishments along the way. This can help to keep you motivated and on track and can also provide you with a sense of accomplishment and satisfaction.

Find an accountability partner: Having an accountability partner, such as a friend, family member, or financial professional, can be a great way to stay motivated and committed to your financial plan. By having someone to report to and share your progress with, you can stay accountable and motivated to achieve your goals.

Stay focused: It can be easy to get sidetracked or lose motivation along the way, but it's important to stay focused on your financial goals. This might involve setting aside dedicated time to work on your financial plan or finding ways to stay motivated and committed, such as reading success stories or seeking support and encouragement from others.

Be persistent: Building wealth and achieving financial independence takes time and effort, and it's important to be persistent in the face of setbacks and challenges. By staying focused and persistent, you can increase your chances of success and achieve your financial goals.

By following these tips, you can stay motivated and committed to your financial plan and increase your chances of success. It is very important to stay motivated and committed to your financial plan in order to achieve your financial goals.

• The Importance of Accountability and Support

Accountability and support can be crucial factors in achieving financial success. By having someone to hold you accountable and provide support and encouragement, you can stay motivated and on track towards achieving your financial goals. Here are some ways that accountability and support can help you to achieve financial success:

Keep you motivated: Having someone to hold you accountable can help to keep you motivated and on track towards achieving your financial goals. Knowing that you have someone checking in on your progress and expecting you to follow through can be a powerful motivator.

Provide a sense of accountability: Having someone to report to and share your progress with can help to create a sense of accountability and can make you more likely to follow through on your financial plan.

Offer guidance and support: Receiving support and guidance from others, such as a financial professional or trusted friend or family member, can help to keep you motivated and on track towards achieving your financial goals. These individuals can provide valuable insights, encouragement, and guidance as you work towards your goals.

Create a sense of community: Surrounding yourself with supportive people who are working towards similar goals can create a sense of community and camaraderie. This can be a great source of motivation and can also provide you with valuable insights and support.

By seeking accountability and support, you can increase your chances of success and stay motivated and on track towards achieving your financial goals. It is very important to have accountability and support in order to achieve your financial goals.

Conclusion

In conclusion, The Frugal Millionaire: Secrets to Building Wealth on a Budget offers a roadmap for achieving financial success and building wealth on a budget. Through a combination of budgeting, investing, building multiple streams of income, and staying motivated and focused, you can increase your chances of financial success and achieve your financial goals.

In this book, we've explored a variety of strategies for building wealth on a budget, including:

Setting clear, specific financial goals and creating a budget to help you stay on track

Cutting expenses and finding ways to save money

Prioritizing your spending and avoiding financial pitfalls

Investing for the long-term and understanding the different types of investments

Building multiple streams of income and finding ways to earn passive income

Staying motivated and focused on your financial goals and overcoming financial setbacks and challenges

Seeking accountability and support to help you stay motivated and committed to your financial plan.

- ## Recap of key points and takeaways

Here are some key points and takeaways from The Frugal Millionaire: Secrets to Building Wealth on a Budget:

Budgeting is an important foundation for building wealth and achieving financial success. By setting clear financial goals and creating a budget, you can stay on track and make the most of your money.

Cutting expenses and finding ways to save money can be a powerful way to build wealth on a budget. By prioritizing your spending and avoiding financial pitfalls, you can increase your chances of success.

Investing for the long-term is an important strategy for building wealth. By understanding the different types of investments and developing a diversified investment portfolio, you can increase your chances of success and achieve your financial goals.

Building multiple streams of income and finding ways to earn passive income can be a powerful way to increase your earning potential and achieve financial independence.

Staying motivated and focused on your financial goals and overcoming financial setbacks and challenges is essential for achieving financial success. By seeking accountability and support, you can stay motivated and on track towards achieving your financial goals.

By following the strategies outlined in this book, you can take control of your financial future and build wealth on a budget. Remember that building wealth is a journey and it takes time, effort, and persistence. With the right strategies and mindset, you can achieve financial success and reach your financial goals.

- ## Encouragement to take action and start building wealth on a budget

Now that you've completed The Frugal Millionaire: Secrets to Building Wealth on a Budget, it's time to take action and start building wealth on a budget. Remember that building wealth is a journey and it takes time, effort, and persistence. By following the strategies outlined in this book and staying motivated and focused on your financial goals, you can increase your chances of success and achieve your financial goals.

Here are some steps you can take t" start building wealth on a budget:

Set clear, specific financial goals: The first step to building wealth on a budget is to set clear, specific financial goals. This means identifying exactly what you want to achieve and setting a timeline for achieving it. By setting specific goals, you can create a roadmap for achieving them and stay motivated along the way.

Create a budget: Once you have set your financial goals, it's important to create a budget that helps you stay on track. This might involve cutting expenses, finding ways to save money, or increasing your income. By creating a budget and sticking to it, you can make the most of your money and increase your chances of success.

Invest for the long-term: Investing for the long-term is an important strategy for building wealth. By understanding the different types of investments and developing a diversified investment portfolio, you can increase your chances of success and achieve your financial goals.

Build multiple streams of income: Building multiple streams of income and finding ways to earn passive income can be a powerful way to increase your earning potential and achieve financial independence.

Seek accountability and support: Having an accountability partner, such as a friend, family member, or financial professional, can be a great way to stay motivated and committed to your financial plan. By seeking support and guidance from others, you can increase your chances of success and stay on track towards achieving your financial goals.

- ## Final thoughts on the benefits of living a frugal and financially responsible lifestyle

In The Frugal Millionaire: Secrets to Building Wealth on a Budget, we've explored the benefits of living a frugal and financially responsible lifestyle and how it can help you to build wealth on a budget. Here are some final thoughts on the benefits of living a frugal and financially responsible lifestyle:

Frugality can help you to make the most of your money: By living a frugal lifestyle, you can stretch your dollars further and make the most of your money. This can be especially important if you're working to build wealth on a budget.

Frugality can help you to achieve financial independence: By living a frugal lifestyle, you can save more money and increase your chances of achieving financial independence. This can be especially important if you're working to build multiple streams of income or achieve financial independence.

Frugality can help you to live a simpler, more fulfilling life: By living a frugal lifestyle, you can focus on the things that matter most to you and live a simpler, more fulfilling life. This can be especially important if you're working to achieve financial independence and build wealth on a budget.

Frugality can help you to be more financially responsible: By living a frugal lifestyle, you can become more financially responsible and make better financial decisions. This can be especially important if you're working to build wealth on a budget and achieve financial independence.

In conclusion, living a frugal and financially responsible lifestyle can be a powerful way to build wealth on a budget and achieve financial independence. By following the strategies outlined in The Frugal Millionaire: Secrets to Building Wealth on a Budget and staying motivated and focused on your financial goals, you can increase your chances of success and achieve your financial goals.

www.ingramcontent.com/pod-product-compliance
Lightning Source LLC
Chambersburg PA
CBHW070313220526
45465CB00004B/1855